super **hot drinks**

super hot
drinks

michael van straten

MITCHELL BEAZLEY

For Alf, a strong man, a good friend, and the best father-in-law ever. I'll keep
my promise, Alf. I'll look after her.

Super Hot Drinks

by Michael van Straten

First published in Great Britain in 2004 by
Mitchell Beazley, an imprint of Octopus Publishing
Group Limited, 2–4 Heron Quays, London E14 4JP.

A CIP catalogue record for this book is available from the British Library.

ISBN: 1 84000 7729

The author and publishers will be grateful for any information that will assist them in keeping
future editions up-to-date. Although all reasonable care has been taken in the preparation of this
book, neither the publishers, editors nor the author can accept any liability for any consequences
arising from the use thereof, or the information contained therein.

Commissioning Editor: Rebecca Spry
Executive Art Editor: Yasia Williams
Editor: Jamie Ambrose
Photographer: Peter Cassidy
Stylist: Louise Mackaness
Proofreader: Diona Gregory
Production: Seyhan Esen
Index: John Noble

Typeset in Myriad MM

Printed and bound by Toppan Printing Company in China

Contents

Introduction

Mention hot drinks and most people's thoughts turn instantly to tea or coffee. There's no doubt that both beverages have played important roles in the social fabric of many nations. From the tea houses of Japan to London's eighteenth-century coffee houses; from the delicately perfumed teas of China to rich Viennese coffees, these drinks have influenced both design and lifestyles around the globe.

Yet in spite of their comforting, stimulating, and health-giving properties (of tea in particular), these are not the world's only enjoyable hot drinks – as this book shows. In it, I have tried to provide the widest possible range of familiar, unusual, and quite frankly surprising ingredients, combinations of which result in warming beverages that can certainly be drunk for pleasure, but that also have some very specific medicinal benefits.

This approach is nothing new. Herb teas, or tisanes, have been used worldwide for thousands of years for therapeutic reasons. The rainforest Indians of Brazil, for example, roast and dry seeds of the guarana plant, then bake it into a stick to take on their travels, together with an extraordinarily effective grater fashioned from the palate bone of a large Amazonian fish called the *piracu*. A gourd filled with boiling water into which some of the stick has been grated produces instant guarana tea. This beverage is both energizing and an appetite suppressant, and helps keep them going on long hunting trips.

Closer to home, simple camomile tea is ideal for the sleepless, fractious child with a temperature or headache. Sage tea relieves sore throats and helps stimulate the flow of milk in breastfeeding mothers. A sprig of fresh mint in a glass of boiling water makes the refreshing tea that is so popular in the Middle East and is the best of all remedies for indigestion. Fresh ginger in a glass of boiling water makes the ultimate remedy for travel sickness or early morning sickness in pregnancy.

But why just stick to teas, when a smoothie of, say, dates, milk, and coconut milk will boost your vitality, or a mug of rum punch with ginger, cinnamon, lemons, and honey will warm you on the coldest of winter days? Such recipes are also included here. A cup of hot chocolate, for instance, with star anise and toasted almonds will help improve your natural resistance to winter coughs and colds.

Warming hot drinks other than coffee and tea were also traditionally part of sick-room medicine, and as you'll see in the relevant chapter, these are often more like soups than drinks. Such recipes include pea, mint, and onion vegetable broth, or beetroot juice and horseradish, which will help to stimulate the circulation, pep up the vitality, and hasten your recovery from illness.

As well as their specific health-enhancing benefits, many of the drinks in this book will also help improve your overall nutrition. You'll drink calcium, protein, B vitamins, and iron from a hot banana smoothie, for example, or plenty of healing betacarotene from a cup of mango mixed with hot chillies.

Of course, no one will like every recipe in this book, but trust me: even the most bizarre-sounding combinations will surprise you. Many aspects of our lives are all too easily bogged down in the rut of routine and habit, and our attitudes to food and drink are no exception. You will look at some of these recipes and your instant reaction will be disbelief that anyone could imagine drinking such combinations. Be adventurous. Open your mind and your taste buds to the concept of new sensations, and be prepared to taste them without prejudice. Over the years, I've suggested most of these to my patients for therapeutic reasons and even I have been surprised at how few people have come back and said once was enough.

And just so you know: while writing this book, my wife Sally and I not only tried and tasted every single recipe ourselves, but we inflicted them on neighbours, friends, and family – whether they needed them or not – just so we could establish a degree of acceptance. The result? The majority of people not only liked but genuinely enjoyed most of the recipes you'll find in the following pages. So take heart; they're all great to drink for pleasure, but if you should have need of their medicinal properties, they'll do you good into the bargain.

War

Warming drinks are emotionally comforting as well as physically protective, curative, and restorative. In this chapter you'll find some surprising, and what may at times even seem to be bizarre, combinations of flavours and textures. Yet every ingredient in every recipe serves a purpose. There are spices such as cloves, cinnamon, and ginger, which boost the circulation and comfort the spirits. There are herbs such as sage, which is a powerful antiseptic and the best treatment for sore throats; mint, which promotes better digestion; elderflowers, which fight

ming

Drinks

viral infections; and garlic, which is a universal winter cure-all.
They're all here, combined in delicious mixtures with health-giving
fruits such as apples, or wonderful protective vegetables such as leeks,
carrots, turnips, and onions to bring sunshine back to your life in the
depths of winter. And for those with a sweeter tooth, I've included a
hot chocolate like you've never tasted, a fruity mulled wine to lift
the lowest of spirits, and even an exotic Brazilian punch that
will get your feet tapping to the rhythms of salsa.

Apple Tea

Just the smell of a traditional English Cox's orange pippin makes you think of warm and mellow fruitfulness as summer turns gently into autumn. Amazingly, French scientists have shown that simply inhaling the aromatic perfume of most apples is enough to lower your blood pressure. Add cloves – that warming, traditional winter spice – and the combination is irresistible.

Serves 2

3 apples, preferably Cox's orange pippins
4 whole cloves
about 425ml or 15 fl oz water

1 Wash the apples and cut them into rough cubes.
2 Put the apple pieces into a saucepan, along with the cloves.
3 Cover with water.
4 Simmer for thirty minutes.
5 Sieve and serve, thinning with more boiling water if necessary.

vital statistics

Apples provide valuable **vitamin C** and are also a rich source of the soluble fibre known as pectin. They also contain **malic** and **tartaric acids**, which help the **digestive** process, while the fibre ensures regularity. This versatile fruit is also an **excellent** food to help relieve the symptoms of gout, **arthritis** and rheumatism. The **essential oil** in cloves is a digestive aid, and this fragrant spice is also pain-relieving and **mood-enhancing**.

Pear and Elderflower Toddy

Ripe pears must be one of the most aromatic of all fruits and, depending on variety, one of the sweetest and juiciest, too. The heady flavour of the fruit lingers on the palate, thanks to its thickness, so if you're buying pear juice for this recipe, make sure you choose a natural, unfiltered brand (one of the cloudy ones) for maximum enjoyment. The use of elderflowers in country wine- and cordial-making has an ancient history, and the combination of these two flavours will soon become a family favourite.

Serves 2

450ml or 16 fl oz pear juice; make your own or use a good organic commercial brand

2 elderflower heads, or 50ml or 2 fl oz diluted elderflower cordial

1. Pour the pear juice into a saucepan.
2. If using elderflower heads, wash them lightly and add them to the pan, flower-side down, along with 50ml (2 fl oz) of water.
3. Bring the mixture slowly to a simmer and keep simmering for five minutes.
4. Remove the flower heads and serve.
5. If using elderflower cordial, add to the warm pear juice and heat through.

vital statistics

Commercial elderflower cordial is, of course, convenient to use, but **elderflowers** are easily available for **free** in many suburban and inner-city parks and certainly in country hedgerows – although you should not pick it by a road. It's **easy** to make enough cordial in the spring to last you the rest of the year; you'll find a recipe for it in most country cookbooks. **Pears** are rich in soluble **fibre,** making them an **excellent** remedy for **chronic** or occasional **constipation**.

Eggy Chocolate

I'm sure that, like me, you are utterly fed up with the self-appointed know-alls who keep saying that all the foods we love are bad for us. Chocolate is one of the prime victims. But here's the good news: in modest amounts, chocolate is actually good for you. The theobromine it contains is one of nature's feel-good chemicals, which is why most of us get a buzz out of eating it. The smooth, velvety texture of this sumptuous drink is not to be missed.

Serves 2
60g or 2¼ oz organic plain chocolate
500ml or 18 fl oz milk
1 egg yolk
2 tsp golden caster sugar

1 Break the chocolate into pieces.
2 Put the milk in a saucepan and heat gently. Add the chocolate and stir until dissolved.
3 Beat the egg yolk with the sugar and add to the chocolate milk.
4 Bring quickly to the boil and serve immediately.

vital statistics

This is a wonderful source of **iron**, **magnesium**, small amounts of **B vitamins**, and some **protein**. The milk makes it **rich** in **calcium** and a useful bedtime drink, because it encourages the **brain's** production of sleep-inducing **tryptophan**.

Fruity Mulled Wine

The brandy in this drink is optional and without it, this is a perfect winter warmer for children. For all its festive feel, it also makes a great everyday drink, especially when those first frosts bring a nip to the air. It is also a valuable protective mixture, which helps boost natural immunity and is particularly good for the heart and circulation.

Serves 8

1 x 75cl or 26 fl oz bottle red grape juice
850ml or 30 fl oz apple juice
60g or 2¼ oz caster sugar
half a stick of cinnamon
85g or 3 oz mixed berries
   (fresh or frozen, not dried)
1 tbsp brandy, optional

1 Put the juices, sugar, and cinnamon into a large saucepan.
2 Heat gently until the sugar is dissolved.
3 Remove mixture from the heat and let it rest for ten minutes.
4 Add the fruit and heat gently for five minutes.
5 If using frozen fruit, continue heating for a further five minutes.
6 Stir in the brandy, if using, and serve.

vital statistics

The powerful **antioxidants** in red grape juice help protect every cell in your body, but most notably they have **anti-cancer** and **heart-protective** properties. The mixed berries not only deliver a huge dose of **vitamin C**, but they, too, are **bursting** with antioxidants, which also do a great job at **protecting** the skin from **ageing**.

Brazil Milk

This might sound like something you'd never dream of trying, but trust me: it's as delicious as it is nourishing. Even for those who like ordinary milk, adding soya to your regular diet is a healthy thing to do – especially for women. In parts of the world where soya is a daily food, women suffer far less breast cancer, menopausal problems, and osteoporosis.

Serves 2
8 Brazil nuts
500ml or 18 fl oz soya milk

1 Crush the Brazil nuts in a small blender or food processor.
2 Reserving one tablespoon of the nuts, put the rest in a saucepan, along with the soya milk.
3 Bring slowly to a simmer.
4 Serve with the reserved nuts scattered on top.

vital statistics
Selenium is a vital mineral which few people get enough of in their daily diets. It's of particular importance to **men**, as it's essential for **protection** against **prostate cancer**. Brazil nuts are an extremely **rich** source, and each cup of this drink provides a day's dose, which is also important in the prevention of **heart** and **circulatory diseases**.

St John's Punch

Variations of this warming punch are served all over Brazil – strangely, on one of the hottest days of the year: June 24, the feast of St John. The tang of citrus fruits, the kick of ginger, and the heady aroma of cloves and cinnamon immediately make you think of tropical islands, exotic South America, and all those sensuous dances, such as the tango or salsa. So drink this one up and dance all you like – just don't drive home!

Serves 6

1 unwaxed orange

2 unwaxed lemons

2.5cm or 1-inch stick ginger

600ml or 20 fl oz dark rum

3 cloves

2 cinnamon sticks

2 tbsp runny honey

1 Thinly slice the orange and lemons.
2 Peel the ginger and beat it until it is half-flattened.
3 Put all the ingredients into a saucepan, along with 300ml (10 fl oz) water.
4 Heat until just at simmering point.
5 Strain and serve.

vital statistics

Just what you need as a winter warmer on a dull, damp, depressing, December afternoon. There's **vitamin C** to ward off winter colds, ginger to heat the **blood**, cloves for the **relief** of **stiff** and **aching joints**, and honey to **soothe sore throats** and chests. The rum is the ultimate bonus – it helps to **revive** flagging spirits.

Veggie Mug

I know this sounds like a soup, but then what *is* soup if it isn't a hot drink? What you're actually getting here is a clear, reviving, and invigorating bouillon and also the basic recipe for great vegetable stock. Once you've made it, you won't want those horrible, salty stock cubes. It's perfect for freezing as ice-cubes, so you can easily defrost however many you need to make an instant hot drink.

Serves 6

1 leek, thoroughly washed, but green part retained

1 carrot, large, washed – and peeled if not organic

1 turnip, washed

1 onion, large, with its skin

6 large stems of parsley

3 sprigs of mint

1 Put all the ingredients into a large stockpot.
2 Add 850 ml (30 fl oz) of water.
3 Bring to a boil, then simmer for one hour.
4 Strain off the vegetables to serve.

vital statistics

This certainly counts as one of your five portions of fruit or veg a day and has a wide range of **health benefits**. Leeks provide **antibacterial** and **antifungal** protection and help ward off chest infections. **Betacarotene** from the carrots is good for the **eyes**. Parsley helps get rid of **excessive fluid**, and the fresh mint brings instant **relief** from indigestion.

Prote

We're constantly being told that prevention is better than cure, so what more appropriate way to prevent illness than by using the abundant protection nature provides to boost our own immune defences? People are quite willing to accept the idea that taking a tiny dose of aspirin every day can protect against strokes and heart disease, but they seem to find it more difficult to understand that there are highly protective foods which could achieve equally dramatic prevention without any of the risk associated with even a child's dose of aspirin (not that any child under twelve should be given aspirin at all). Many of the deeply coloured fruits and vegetables offer natural cancer protection, and there are herbs and spices that protect against digestive problems, loss of concentration, and general fatigue.

ctive

Drinks

There are nutrients that take care of your eyes and significantly reduce the risk of deteriorating eyesight and even blindness in old age. There are even delicious foods that will make it less likely that you'll develop joint problems such as rheumatism, arthritis or gout. The sad truth is that most people find prevention a difficult concept, and they're not prepared to take action until things go wrong. Of course, I can't guarantee that if you use these drinks you won't develop any of the associated conditions; conversely, if you do use them and don't get sick, it's impossible to prove cause and effect. However, if you don't use them and you get ill, you could be too late. So why take the risk? All I'm suggesting are some very enjoyable but slightly different hot drinks which certainly can't hurt – and ultimately may help.

Hot, Hot Chocolate

Isn't it great to discover that one of your favourite foods – which you always thought of as sinful and unhealthy – is suddenly considered good for you? That's certainly the case with chocolate, as long as you stick to modest quantities and use the best possible quality. Not only does chocolate contain feel-good chemicals that lift your mood, it's also a rich source of protective antioxidants. So it's official: you can enjoy this drink with a clear conscience.

Serves 1

1 heaped tsp organic chocolate powder

300ml or 10 fl oz full-cream Jersey milk

1cm or ½ inch cinnamon stick

1 In a mug, mix the chocolate powder with two teaspoons of the milk.
2 Bring the rest of the milk to a boil in a saucepan.
3 Pour into the mug containing the chocolate mixture.
4 Stir and serve with the cinnamon stick floating on top.

vital statistics

Using quality chocolate with a minimum seventy per cent cocoa solids content, you'll get reasonable amounts of the minerals **iron** and **magnesium** as well as the natural chemical **theobromine**, the constituent that triggers the release of **good-mood** chemicals from the brain. There's now ample evidence to show that feeling **happy** and **positive** gives a substantial boost to the **immune system** and helps protect the body against **infection** and disease. Add the **calcium** from the milk and you get added protection against **osteoporosis**.

Cranberry Cup

Many people think that hot fruit juices are rather strange, although they have no qualms at all about hot punches or mulled wine. Fruit juices are no different – except, of course, that they don't contain alcohol. Apart from tasting amazingly good, this mixture of cranberry juice and star anise is doubly protective because it's hot. Served cold, the essential oils from the star anise would not be extracted, so you'd get neither the benefit nor much flavour.

Serves 2
4 whole star anise
300ml or 10 fl oz cranberry juice

1 In a medium saucepan, add the star anise to the cranberry juice.
2 Bring slowly to just under boiling point.
3 Leave the star anise floating on top to serve.

vital statistics

The **protective** properties of cranberry juice are legendary, and there surely can't be a **woman** in the Western world who doesn't know that the juice of this amazing berry is both a **treatment** for and a protector against **urinary infections**. It does the same job for **men**, too, although it's less common for them to suffer from these problems. Star anise is **rich** in essential oils like **estragol** and **anethole**, which improve digestion, protect against flatulence, and help the appetite. They also **protect** against coughs, **colds**, and catarrh.

Gingered-up Beetroot

This is another extremely protective drink that sounds a bit bizarre. But before you turn up your nose and turn over the page, try it and you'll be pleasantly surprised. It tastes like slightly spicy, bubbly borscht (the traditional Eastern European beetroot soup). This is a blood and circulation mixture which protects against fatigue, loss of concentration, and many forms of cancer.

Serves 2
400ml or 14 fl oz beetroot juice
4 drops ginger essence
100ml or 3½ fl oz ginger ale

1 In a medium saucepan, heat the beetroot juice until just boiling.
2 Pour into two mugs and add two drops of ginger essence to each.
3 Top up with ginger ale, and serve.

vital statistics

Beetroot is far more than the insipid stuff so often used in salads in the UK. The red colouring carries specific **anti-carcinogens** attached to its molecules, and it also more than doubles the amount of **oxygen** the body cells are able to absorb. This juice will **boost** natural **resistance**, **protect** convalescents from relapse, and act as a valuable **aid** to good digestion. It's a mild **liver stimulant**, too, so helps in the digestion of fats. Adding the ginger boosts the **circulation** and also helps improve **digestion**.

Black Beauty

Since the earliest wild horses roamed our planet, they have been symbols of strength, speed, and beauty – and this unusual hot toddy, named after those beasts, will help keep you strong, healthy, and vital. The American Concord grape – so deep-purple it's almost black – is one of the most powerful antioxidant and protective foods, so this drink is a major weapon in the fight against free radicals that accelerate ageing and damage the body's cells. Cinnamon, cloves, and allspice are antibacterial and antiviral, and will help protect you against winter infections. The bonus comes from the nutmeg, which contains a mild hallucinogen called myristicin that lifts the mood.

Serves 2

750ml or 26 fl oz American Concord
  purple grape juice
1 cinnamon stick
a generous grating of nutmeg
a pinch of allspice
10 whole cloves
1 unwaxed lime
1 unwaxed orange
15ml or ½ fl oz molasses
2 sprigs of curry plant

1 Put the grape juice into a stainless-steel, glass or enamel (not aluminium) pan, then add the cinnamon, nutmeg, and allspice.
2 Press the cloves into the lime and add to the juice.
3 Remove as much of the peel from the orange as possible, leaving the pith behind.
4 Cut the peel into very thin strips and add to the pan, along with the juice of the orange.
5 Heat slowly, stirring in the molasses when the liquid starts to simmer.
6 Keep simmering gently for ten minutes.
7 Put a sprig of curry plant into two large, heatproof glasses, then strain this delicious, invigorating, alcohol-free punch into each.

vital statistics

This drink is bursting with protective **antioxidants**, and the orange peel is high in **bioflavonoids** (natural substances that protect the **heart** and circulatory system). You'll also get a big boost of **vitamin C** from the lime and orange juice, as well as important levels of **carotenoids** (natural pigments from reddish-yellow plants) – **essential** for skin and eye health. Thanks to the molasses, there are useful doses of **trace minerals** that your body needs on a daily basis.

Mulled Pawpaw

This is truly super protection in a glass. A large punch-bowlful, served to your friends before dinner will give them all a glow of well-being – and that's without any alcohol. You could, of course, always add some white rum if you wanted something a little stronger. Like many tropical fruits, the pawpaw is rich in protective enzymes and vitamins, and when combined with these tropical spices, it provides a huge boost to the immune system.

Serves 10

10 cloves
1 cinnamon stick, broken into 3 pieces
150g or 5½oz demerara sugar
1 litre or 35 fl oz pawpaw juice
1 litre or 35 fl oz apple juice
1 tsp allspice
3 pinches of nutmeg
1 small pawpaw

1 Tie the cloves and cinnamon in a muslin bag.
2 Put the sugar and juices into a large saucepan.
3 Add the muslin bag, allspice, and nutmeg.
4 Bring slowly to the boil and simmer for ten minutes.
5 Fish out the muslin bag.
6 Deseed and peel the pawpaw and cut into thin slices.
7 Serve in a punch-bowl or other large, heatproof bowl with the fruit slices floating on top.

vital statistics

An average pawpaw provides twice your daily requirement of **vitamin C** and a quarter of the **vitamin A**. Both these nutrients are essential for the proper functioning of your immune system and **natural defences**. For this reason alone, the recipe is a super protector. Additional **nutrients** from the pawpaw and apple juices, the **immune-boosting** properties of cinnamon and allspice, and the **feel-good factor** from nutmeg push this drink to the top of the protective list.

Hot Bloody Mary

It's not often that any form of processing increases the protective value of fresh produce, but this is definitely true of tomatoes. This juice is hugely protective against prostate and breast cancer, and it also helps prevent age-related macular degeneration (AMD), the most common cause of blindness in the elderly. With or without the vodka, this is a really delicious drink with huge health benefits.

Serves 2

300ml or 10 fl oz tomato juice
2 dashes Tabasco sauce
2 small measures vodka
   (about 15ml or 1 tbsp)
2 cinnamon sticks

1 Warm the tomato juice and pour it into two decorative, heatproof glasses.
2 Add the Tabasco sauce and vodka.
3 Serve immediately, with the cinnamon sticks for stirring.

vital statistics

Fully ripe tomatoes are the richest source of the carotenoid **lycopene**. Unfortunately, many commercially produced tomatoes are harvested early and artificially ripened, so they contain far less of this **essential nutrient**. When canned or juiced, extremely ripe tomatoes are used, and the lycopene content is also **concentrated** by the processing. This guarantees the maximum intake of this unique nutrient that **protects** against **prostate** and **breast cancers**, heart disease, and **eye** problems.

Aztec Dream

To the Aztecs, chocolate was so precious that only royal families were allowed to drink it. It isn't hard to see why; besides its wonderful taste, chocolate contains valuable antioxidant and other protective substances. Here, it is combined with cardamom and star anise, which also protect against chest infections, sore throats, and sinus problems, while soya milk's natural plant hormones help strengthen bones – vital protection against osteoporosis. Hot chocolate will never be the same again.

Serves 2

300ml or 10 fl oz organic dark hot chocolate, prepared according to manufacturer's directions using half full-fat milk and half soya milk

4 cardamom seeds

a sprinkle of ground star anise

15g or ½oz flaked almonds

a generous handful of fresh mint leaves

100g or 3½oz fromage frais

2 sprigs of mint, for garnish

1 Prepare the chocolate in a saucepan, according to the directions on the packet, then add the cardamom seeds and star anise powder.
2 In a dry frying pan, gently heat the almonds until they start to brown and crisp.
3 Put the mint leaves and fromage frais into a blender and whizz until well-combined.
4 Pour the hot chocolate into large mugs, top with the fromage frais, sprinkle with the almonds, and add the sprigs of mint.

vital statistics

As well as all the **B vitamins**, minerals, and **antioxidants** in the organic chocolate, there is **calcium** and the essential **vitamin D** in the full-fat milk. The natural bacteria and extra calcium from the fromage frais, and peppermint **oil** from the mint leaves add extra nutrients and improve digestive absorption, while the almonds are a **rich** source of protective **vitamin E**, zinc, and **selenium**.

Vita

Vitality is a strange concept. You can't weigh it, measure it, count it, or test for it. Yet the minute you meet people, you can tell instantly whether they have it or not. Some say you either have it or you don't, but this is not true; anyone can acquire it. Vitality has two components, however, and you need both if you want to function to your optimal potential. True vitality is a perfect balance between the physical and the psychological. Although the recipes in this chapter provide some aid to mental and emotional vitality, thanks to mood-enhancing and anti-stress and -anxiety ingredients in the drinks, most of this aspect of your life-force must be generated from within. You must develop positive attitudes to life; hackneyed though they may sound, all those old sayings have a certain ring of truth. See your glass as half-full, not half-empty; look for the best in everyone; when one door closes another one opens; every cloud has a

lity
Drinks

silver lining; laugh and the world laughs with you, cry and you cry alone;
put a brave face on things; keep a stiff upper lip… The list is endless.
I realize that these supposedly outmoded attitudes fly in the face of
all of today's politically correct theories, but underlying them is the
promotion of self-esteem, self-reliance – and vitality. As far as the
physical aspects of vitality are concerned, nutrition plays a fundamental
role. For that reason, these drinks improve digestion and your
absorption of vitality-boosting nutrients. They fight infection as well as
helping the body to overcome its loss of vital force caused by illness.
They restore the physiological ability to repair and regenerate damaged
and worn-out cells, and they provide both instant and slow-release
energy to keep you functioning at your vital best during demanding
periods of both physical and mental activity.

Hot Tommy

When you've been laid low by a cold or flu, you're recovering from illness or an operation, or you're just ground down by an extended period of work or stress, this is the drink you need. Packed with vitality, energy, and valuable nutrients, you'll find this tomato-based, almost soup-like beverage an instant shot in the arm. Easily digested and with a savoury tang to please even the most jaded of palates, it will soon be on your list of favourites.

Serves 4

**300ml or 10 fl oz vegetable stock
(*see* recipe for Veggie Mug on page 18
or make it with a low-salt commercial
stock cube)**
200ml or 7 fl oz milk
**1 x 400g or 14 oz can tinned,
crushed tomatoes**
1 large onion, peeled and finely grated
20g or ¾ oz sago

1   Put all the ingredients into a large pot or saucepan.
2   Simmer for one hour.
3   Strain and serve in mugs.

vital statistics

Tomatoes are the richest of all sources of the nutrient **lycopene**. This member of the **carotenoid** family is one of the most protective of all the phytochemicals and will quickly **boost** your lowered vitality. Sago, made from the starchy pith of the sago palm tree, is a quickly digested **energy source**, providing the healthiest form of carbohydrates. **Minerals** from the vegetable stock, and, **calcium** and **B vitamins** from the milk add to the energy-boosting value.

Lemonbalmade

Viral infections are guaranteed to sap your vitality. Whether it's a mild dose of flu, a severe stomach upset or viral pneumonia, the extent to which you feel low doesn't really depend on the severity of the illness. You'll still feel rotten. No matter what sort of virus you've picked up, the three ingredients in this drink will help you beat the infection and regain your lost vitality.

Serves 2

2 large lemons
2 generous sprigs of lemon balm
2 tsp molasses

1 Juice the lemons.
2 Divide the juice between two mugs.
3 Add a sprig of lemon balm to each.
4 Top up with boiling water.
5 Cover and leave for five minutes.
6 Remove the lemon balm and stir in the molasses to serve.

vital statistics

Not only do lemons provide ample amounts of **vitamin C** to help **fight** all **infections**, but lemon balm is one of the few natural **antiviral** plants in the entire herbal repertoire. The natural chemicals in this herb will **tackle** a whole variety of **viruses**, including those responsible for all forms of herpes and chickenpox. The natural sugars and **minerals** in molasses will **supercharge** the vitality-enhancing effect of this drink.

Desert Island Juice

Drinks made from milk have long been associated with growth, health, and vitality. Milk is an excellent source of calcium, protein, B vitamins, and energy from its natural lactose (milk sugar). It is, for most people, one of the most easily digestible of all foods. There are those who have an intolerance to lactose, and others have an allergy to milk protein. But for everyone else, milk – mixed here with health-boosting dates – is a great vitality drink.

Serves 2

8 dates, stoned and ready-to-eat
200ml or 7 fl oz milk
200ml or 7 fl oz coconut milk, or the
equivalent in coconut cream diluted
with hot water to the consistency of
milk – about 4 heaped tsp

1 Cut the dates into eight pieces each. Put into a small bowl and just cover with freshly boiled water.
2 Leave for ten minutes.
3 Purée the dates, with the water, in a small blender until completely smooth.
4 Heat the milk and coconut milk (or cream mixture).
5 Add the puréed dates.
6 Froth with a whisk or cappuccino wand, and serve.

vital statistics

For anyone who can't tolerate dairy milk, this recipe is just as good a vitality **booster** if you make it with soya milk. Dates are a key to the **benefits** of this drink and have been part of man's staple diet since 3,000BC. Some varieties are an extremely **rich** source of **iron**, particularly Gondela from Sudan, and Khidri from Riyadh. All dates are vitality food as their ease of **digestion** and **instant energy** are acceptable to the weakest invalids.

Peanut Butter Surprise

This may sound like a kid's milkshake, but it's great for adults, too. For some reason, to many people, the very thought of peanut butter means bad health, piling on the pounds, and something not to be eaten by sensible adults. Nothing could be further from the truth – especially if you choose organic, low-salt brands. The vitality boost from this drink comes from the combination of instant and slow-release energy.

Serves 2
4 level tbsp smooth peanut butter
300ml or 10 fl oz runny live yoghurt
150ml or 5 fl oz milk
runny honey, to serve (optional)

1 Blend the peanut butter together with about half the yoghurt.
2 Pour into a saucepan with the rest of the yoghurt and the milk.
3 Warm, stirring continuously, until well combined, but don't boil it or you'll kill the good bacteria.
4 Serve in mugs or heatproof glasses. Drizzle over with runny honey, if desired.

vital statistics

Few people realize just how **revitalizing** live yoghurt really is. As well as the easily available calories from the **natural carbohydrate** it contains, the millions of **beneficial** live bacteria have a profound effect on the immune system, boosting your **resistance** and enhancing the conversion of food into energy. Peanuts provide health-giving **lignans**, vitality-boosting mono-unsaturated **fatty acids**, and a bonus of **minerals** and **fibre**.

Get Up and Go Tea

Camomile tea is usually associated with being calming and sedative: which it is. But it's also an extremely effective mood-enhancer and helps stimulate energy and vitality simply because you feel better in yourself. Amaretto, the Italian almond liqueur, adds the most delicious flavour, and the small amount of alcohol is a mood-booster, too.

Serves 1

1 heaped tsp dried camomile flowers or 1 commercially made, preferably organic, camomile tea bag

1 tbsp Amaretto

1 tsp runny honey

1   If using the dried herb, put it into a cup or infuser, pour in about 250ml (9 fl oz) boiling water, cover and leave for ten minutes, then strain or lift out the central part of infuser. If using a tea bag, brew the tea according to the packet's instructions.
2   Add the Amaretto and honey.
3   Stir well and serve.

vital statistics

One of the most frequent causes of a lack of vitality and chronic fatigue is a lack, or poor quality, of sleep. Thanks to the **chamazulene** in camomile, this tea is a **gentle** sleep inducer and helps ensure you **enjoy** all the essential stages of sleep. This means you wake up **refreshed** and full of **vitality**.

Hot and Smooth Prune

I've never managed to understand why the prune is the butt of so many jokes. Yes, it does contain natural chemicals which have a mild laxative effect and that's thanks to a natural chemical called hydroxyphenylisatin. But prunes are far more than this, and combined here with live yoghurt, the juice makes a surprisingly delicious and enjoyable revitalizing drink.

Serves 2
450ml or 16 fl oz prune juice
30ml or 1 fl oz thick-set live yoghurt

1 In a medium saucepan, warm the prune juice gently.
2 Pour into two mugs.
3 Serve with the yoghurt floating on top.

vital statistics

Prunes are truly a majestic fruit. Hugely prized in France, where they originated, they have their own *appellation contrôllée*, Pruneaux d'Agen, just like the finest of wines. Weight for weight, they're by far the **richest** food source of protective **antioxidants** and provide a massive **boost** to **natural resistance** and vitality. Don't wait until you feel you need to use this kitchen remedy; enjoy it when you're at **risk** of being attacked by any bugs around.

Apricot Delight

The thick consistency of this wonderful drink is more reminiscent of nectars than juices. Fortunately, unlike the commercial varieties, there's no added sugar – just the wonderful flavour of apricots, redolent of summertime but available all year round.

Serves 2

12 ready-to-eat, dried apricots

1 Snip the apricots into half the size of a small fingernail.
2 Reserving six pieces, put the rest into a saucepan and cover with 500ml (18 fl oz) cold water.
3 Bring to the boil and simmer gently for fifteen minutes.
4 Leave to cool slightly before liquidizing until smooth.
5 Reheat and serve, with the reserved apricot pieces on top.

vital statistics

Apricots are a wonderful **health-giving** fruit, long prized by the Hunza peoples living in their Himalayan mountain villages. Their legendary **fitness**, vitality, and **longevity** – individuals regularly live to the age of well over 100 – are attributed to their consumption of fresh and dried apricots throughout the year. They offer a perfect balance of instant and slow-release **energy** and are a huge source of vitality-boosting **betacarotene**, essential for immunity, and **healthy skin** and **eyesight**.

Pick-

Most people's idea of a pick-me-up is usually a massive injection of caffeine or a very large hair of the dog. The alternative is an instant sugar fix from a bar of chocolate, a cola drink, a bag of sweets or a couple of chocolate brownies. None of these work. While small amounts of alcohol can provide a gentle boost, anything more than that has a very specific depressive action on the brain and central nervous system. Because this action works mainly on the brain's inhibitory centres, the result is a temporary outward appearance of jollity, energy, and extrovert behaviour. This is followed inevitably by a serious slump and an even worse decline. As far as the sugar fix is concerned, all that happens is that you get trapped into high-low swinging blood-sugar levels. The high feels great, but very soon the low kicks in, with a craving for more sugar – and you're locked into the vicious cycle.

me-up

Drinks

Caffeine is no friendly bedfellow, either, although it's not quite the villain it's often made out to be. Some people are extremely caffeine-sensitive, and one cup of coffee leaves them jittery, anxious, and sweating for the rest of the day. For most of us, though, two or three cups a day can be quite beneficial, but using excessive caffeine-based drinks to lift yourself from the slough of physical weakness and mental or emotional bleakness never works and leaves you coping with tremors, headaches, increased heart rate, and the risk of high blood pressure. The healthy answer lies in these pick-me-up drinks: foods that nourish body and soul and provide energy, whether it's instant or long-term. Here you'll find herbs that boost circulation, improve the blood, stimulate the thyroid, nourish brain cells, and energize the emotions. Some combinations may seem unusual, strange or even outlandish, but they work – *and* they taste good.

Rosemary Milk

Most people wouldn't automatically associate milk with rosemary. After all, they don't quite fit together in the same way as, say, fish and chips or bread and jam. But when you're feeling a bit low, getting over an illness or generally just under the weather, this drink will provide some comfort, calmness, and a feeling of mental alertness.

Serves 1

1 x 15cm or 6-inch stem of rosemary
250ml or 9 fl oz milk

1. Break the rosemary into four pieces.
2. Put three of the pieces into a saucepan and add the milk.
3. Bring slowly to the boil and simmer for five minutes.
4. Press the rosemary against the side of the pan to extract the juices, then discard.
5. Serve with the reserved rosemary floating on top.

vital statistics

Rosemary is known as the herb of **remembrance** – and that's no coincidence. The natural chemicals it contains act as **stimulants** to the areas of the **brain** that control your **memory**, a fact well-known to the ancient Greeks and Romans. The herb is also mood-enhancing, **anti-inflammatory**, antibacterial, and **stimulating**.

Cashew Crunch

The Chinese, South Americans, and native North Americans, as well as the Greeks and Romans, acknowledged the enormous contribution that nuts provide in terms of health and nutrition. They're a great source of slow-release energy to keep you going. Combining them with the instant energy from natural sugars in the coconut milk makes this an unusual and intriguingly flavoured pick-me-up drink.

Serves 2

85g or 3 oz dry-roasted cashew nuts
500ml or 18 fl oz coconut milk

1 Put about two tablespoons of the nuts into a small blender with about four tablespoons of the milk.
2 Whizz until very smooth.
3 Put the rest of the milk into a saucepan and heat gently until just boiling.
4 Add the nut mixture and stir until fully combined.
5 Froth with a whisk or cappuccino wand.
6 Pour into mugs.
7 Crush the reserved nuts and scatter them on top to serve.

vital statistics

Cashews have a high content of **heart-protective** mono-unsaturated **fatty acids**. They're a good source of energy-giving **protein**, folic acid for good blood, all-round **health protection** and plenty of healthy calories. Although coconut milk isn't very nutritious, it's extremely **refreshing**, helping to make this drink welcome when you need a boost after prolonged periods of **stress**.

Mixed Fruit Cup

No matter what's pulling you down at the moment, here's a drink that is not only warming, but an instant antidote when you're in need of a pick-me-up. Whether you're run down after illness or infection, worn out by demanding physical activity due to work or exercise, or just feeling thoroughly toxic after a night on the town, this delicately flavoured and wonderfully healthy drink will soon help you back to top form.

Serves 4

4 satsumas
350ml or 12 fl oz apple juice
2 green tea bags
1 unwaxed lemon

1 Juice the satsumas and put the juice into a medium saucepan.
2 Add the apple juice and heat gently.
3 Make 300ml or 18 fl oz of tea using the tea bags, following the packet's instructions.
4 Add the hot tea to the warm juices.
5 Slice the lemon thinly and serve the tea in mugs with the lemon slices on top.

vital statistics

Of course, there's masses of **vitamin C** in this drink – as long as you heat the juice gently and don't let it boil. The **soluble fibre** pectin and other **natural chemicals** in the apple juice help eliminate toxic residues, and green tea is one of the most potent of the **immune-boosting** drinks.

Pep Up with Peppermint

The sharp, almost astringent flavour of peppermint is a real eye-opener. There are, of course, many varieties of mint, probably the most popular of all culinary herbs. But peppermint has the most distinctive and unmistakable flavour. The bite of this mint tea, softened with the soothing flavour of honey, is a wonderful anytime mood-booster.

Serves 1

3 large sprigs of peppermint
1 tbsp runny honey

1 Wash the mint and put it into a jug.
2 Cover with 250ml or 9 fl oz of boiling water.
3 Leave to infuse for ten minutes.
4 Strain the tea into a mug.
5 Add the honey and stir briskly until dissolved.

vital statistics

The essential oils of **menthol** and **menthone** are found in all varieties of mint, whether it's apple mint, ginger mint, Moroccan mint or any of the dozens of their relatives. Mint is most commonly thought of as a **digestive** remedy – which indeed it is – but the **powerful** peppermint is also **mood-enhancing** and **protective** against infections.

Apricot Get Up and Go

There's nothing like a glass of wine when body and soul need a bit of a lift. Strictly speaking, alcohol is a depressant, but in small amounts it depresses the brain's inhibitory centres, helping you feel more confident, livelier, and more vibrantly active. The sweetness of the apricots and the bitter-sweet taste of molasses complement each other perfectly.

Serves 3
350g or 12 oz fresh apricots
2 tbsp molasses
50ml or 2 fl oz dry white wine

1 Wash, stone, and quarter the apricots.
2 Put them in a saucepan with the molasses and 500ml or 18 fl oz of water.
3 Stew until soft.
4 While still hot, liquidize until smooth.
5 Add the wine and give the mixture another quick burst in the blender or food processor.
6 Pour into mugs and serve.

vital statistics

Instant **energy** from the natural sugars in apricots and molasses, the satisfying and **sustaining** consistency of liquidized apricots, and the **gentle lift** from the small amount of alcohol make this a great mid-morning booster or an ideal early-evening **pick-me-up** when it's hard to raise enthusiasm for your pre-arranged evening out.

Kiwi and Guarana Cup

Kiwi fruit is amazingly good value these days. I'm really pleased to see that it has come so far from the times when it was used almost exclusively as decoration for fruit flans; you simply couldn't appreciate the flavour when it was overpowered by so many other ingredients. Juiced, however, kiwi fruit basks in its own glory: beautiful colour, fabulous flavour, and in the A-team as far as nutrients go. I'll admit I'd never tried warm kiwi fruit until I started this book. Now I'm a firm fan – and I know you will be, too.

Serves 2

home-juiced kiwi-fruit juice (you'll need 6–8) or 500ml or 18 fl oz commercially made variety

2 tsp guarana (if you can't find loose powder, break up about 4 pills)

1 kiwi fruit

1 Put the juice and guarana into a medium saucepan and heat gently.
2 Pour into two mugs. Slice the extra kiwi fruit and perch one slice on the edge of each mug to serve.

vital statistics

To the rainforest tribes on the Brazilian Amazon, guarana is known as the energy seed of the forest – and for good reason. The tribal hunters use this amazing plant to **sustain** them and boost their **energy levels** on their long trips in the most awful conditions of unbearable heat and unimaginable humidity. Kiwi fruit is a **rich** source of protective **vitamin C** and also contains significant amounts of **potassium**, which is so important for sustained **muscle** activity.

Chicken Yum-Yum

This may look like a soup, smell like a soup, and taste like a soup – that's because it *is* a soup, and what could be more of a pick-me-up than a mug full of this crystal-clear, energizing, warming, and immune-boosting chicken broth? In different cultures around the world, from traditional Jewish villages in frozen Siberia to the steamy humidity of the Far East, the burning heat of India or the plains of China, chicken broth functions like Jupiter: the bringer of jollity.

Serves 3

1 chicken quarter (not a breast)
1 leek, washed and quartered
1 fennel bulb, quartered
1 large handful of mixed summer herbs
1 carrot, sliced lengthways
1 onion, halved, with skin left on
850ml or 30 fl oz water

1 Trim any fat off the chicken.
2 Add the vegetables and water.
3 Simmer, covered, for forty minutes.
4 Strain off the chicken and vegetables.
5 Serve the yum-yum immediately.

This can be kept in the refrigerator for up to three days. If you do this, skim off any residue of cold fat and heat on a stove or in a microwave before serving.

vital statistics

Root vegetables are an abundant source of minerals, **carotenoids**, and other **phytochemicals**. Although most of the vitamin C is lost during the prolonged cooking, nearly all the other **nutrients** end up in the soup, together with the **immune-boosting** and **antiviral** components from the chicken.

Circu

Circulatory problems come in many guises. They can be caused by obesity, sedentary lifestyles, diabetes, narrowing of the arteries, high blood pressure, raised cholesterol, heart disease or kidney problems. Chronic constipation can also disrupt your circulation, as it causes varicose veins, which lead to varicose ulcers, which can take months, sometimes years, to heal. Prolonged physical pressure in patients confined to beds or wheelchairs can restrict the blood flow, causing pressure sores, which are also extremely difficult to heal. In addition to all these factors, smoking, excessive alcohol, large amounts of caffeine, and Raynaud's syndrome can all cause narrowing of the tiny blood vessels at the end of the circulatory tree, leading to excruciatingly painful 'dead' fingers and toes. In the worst possible scenario, gangrene and amputation are often the tragic result. Even apparently unconnected

lation

Drinks

problems such as vertigo, headaches, migraine, and tinnitus can be triggered by reductions in the efficiency of blood flow. This whole area of circulatory inefficiency is one in which self-help can often be as effective as medical intervention – especially if you start early, at the first sign of any symptoms. Of course, serious conditions will need to be treated by your own physician, but using some of these simple remedies will certainly make you feel more comfortable and may enable your doctor to prescribe lower doses of certain medicines which could have side effects. Apart from all these rather dire symptoms and conditions, your circulation may just be in need of a boost because it's cold or you're just a bit run down or anaemic. In these cases, the hot drinks in this chapter will work wonders and very quickly get the blood rushing round your system.

Oranges and Lemons

All citrus-fruit juices protect and improve the circulation, thanks to their exceptionally high vitamin C content. Adding some rind helps to protect the integrity and strength of the walls of both arteries and veins. There is also an additional benefit in the enormous increase in natural immune resistance, which is necessary to fight off everyday infections such as coughs, colds, and flu.

Serves 2
4 unwaxed oranges
1 unwaxed large lemon
30ml or 1 fl oz orange blossom water

1 Juice the oranges and lemon and take two curls of both orange and lemon rind.
2 Mix the juices together and heat gently in a saucepan until just simmering.
3 Pour into two heatproof glasses.
4 Divide the orange-blossom water and rind curls between the glasses to serve.

vital statistics

Apart from being an immune-booster, **vitamin C** has many valuable properties. Most importantly, it's one of the most powerful **antioxidants**, helping to **protect** individual **cells** from damage and making it vital for the protection of the entire circulatory system. The **bioflavonoids** in the peel and pith improve your absorption of vitamin C and have their own **strengthening** effect on the walls of **blood vessels**.

Hot Chilli Mango

Now we're really getting down to the nitty-gritty of circulation-boosters. The hot chilli sauce will get the blood fairly whizzing round your circulatory system, and the taste is less fiery than you'd expect, thanks to the soothing sweetness of the mango. This is the perfect drink when you come in from a brisk winter's walk, a frosty afternoon's leaf-sweeping or a cold morning on the edge of a sports field while the kids compete; if you've got any sense, you'll take a flask with you.

Serves 2

500ml or 18 fl oz home-pressed mango juice (or a good commercial variety)
2 tsp hot chilli sauce

1 Put both ingredients into a saucepan.
2 Heat until just boiling.
3 Serve immediately in mugs or heatproof glasses.

vital statistics

The history of the mango goes back to at least 2,000BC, when it was used by Ayurvedic doctors in its native India. It contains **masses** of **vitamins A**, **C**, and **E**, together with **potassium** and **iron**, making it a super-protector of the **heart** and circulatory system. The hot South American chillies contain the circulatory stimulant **capsaicin**. Within moments of enjoying this drink, the tiny **blood vessels** dilate, your **skin** flushes, and you're suffused with a warm and **comforting** glow.

Beetroot Bopper

Throughout Eastern Europe, beetroot has been used for centuries as a blood tonic, and even as a treatment for leukaemia. It is reputed to improve the oxygen-carrying capacity of blood, making the circulation more efficient. Surprisingly, the combination of beetroot and horseradish is widely used as a pickle-type condiment in Eastern Europe, and the flavours are just brilliant together.

Serves 2

**1 tsp freshly grated horseradish
  (or use a strong commercial variety)**
500ml or 18 fl oz beetroot juice

1 Whizz the horseradish in a blender with 125ml or 4 fl oz of the beetroot juice.
2 Put the rest of the juice into a saucepan.
3 Add the blended horseradish and stir until well combined.
4 Heat gently until just boiling.
5 Pour into mugs and serve.

vital statistics

Beetroot was considered to be food of the gods by the ancient Greeks, and was equally valued by the true European Romanies for its **circulatory benefits**. The root contains specific **cancer-fighting chemicals**, so we should all be consuming beetroot on a regular basis. Horseradish is one of the great circulatory **stimulants**, containing a chemical called **sinigrin**, which not only speeds up the circulation, but when crushed is converted into a powerful **antibacterial** called allylisothiocyanate.

Hot Banana Smoothie

There's something very comforting about this combination of bananas, milk, and cocoa, which gets its hidden punch and flavour from the added cinnamon. This drink not only helps improve circulation, it also protects against heart disease and high blood pressure, and will even relieve the distress of PMS.

Serves 2

2 small bananas, peeled
300ml or 10 fl oz milk
125ml or 4 fl oz live yoghurt
1 heaped tsp mixed cocoa powder and
    ground cinnamon

1 Put the first three ingredients into a blender and whizz until very smooth.
2 Pour into a saucepan and heat gently until just simmering.
3 Use a cappuccino wand or whisk to stir up a froth.
4 Pour into two mugs or heatproof glasses and serve with cocoa powder scattered on top.

vital statistics

Bananas are rich in **potassium**, which is important for normal heart function and for the prevention of **high blood pressure**, making them a circulatory superfood. Thanks to their high content of **vitamin B$_6$**, and their ability to prevent **fluid retention**, they also help reduce the distressing and uncomfortable symptoms of PMS. Add the **theobromine** in the cocoa and **volatile oils** from the cinnamon, and it won't be long before you're glowing.

Slemp

A favourite from Holland, this is drunk by everyone who has managed (or can still manage) to get their skates on and go for a stimulating winter race along frozen canals between the dykes. They return with cheeks aglow, healthily out of puff, and ready for this drink to get them warm and add to the circulation boost of a few hours' exercise in the fresh air. The spices are the biggest stimulant.

Serves 6

4cm or 1½ inches cinnamon stick

2 strands of saffron

3 cloves

1 nutmeg, cut in half

1 tbsp dried green tea

850ml or 30 fl oz milk

1 unwaxed lemon

¼ tsp salt

sugar (preferably golden caster sugar) to taste

1 Tie the spices and tea in a piece of muslin.
2 Put the milk into a saucepan and add the muslin bag.
3 Finely grate the peel of the lemon and add to the pan, along with the salt.
4 Simmer gently for one hour.
5 Remove the spice bag.
6 Pour into mugs and let everyone sweeten to taste.

vital statistics

Essential oils such as **saffronal** and **crocins** from the saffron, **myristicin** from nutmeg, **cinnamaldehyde** from cinnamon, and **eugenol** from the cloves are all circulation **stimulants**, and the **antioxidants** in green tea make this drink powerfully **protective**. Apart from these chemical actions, the mellow, spicy flavours are **warming** on their own.

Sorrel Tea

This tea is one of the favourite tonics of the herbalist. Roman soldiers used to eat such wild sorrel when they were marching, as it was said to stop them feeling thirsty, and the earliest Roman physicians knew that it helped the body get rid of surplus fluid. In the time of Henry VIII, it was a highly prized vegetable which the king adored, and his doctors used it as one of the earliest spring blood tonics.

Serves 1
1 large handful fresh sorrel leaves
runny honey

1. Wash the sorrel and tear roughly.
2. Put in a mug or infuser and cover with 250ml or 9 fl oz of boiling water.
3. Cover and leave for ten minutes.
4. Strain and sweeten with honey.

vital statistics

Sorrel is believed by herbalists to both improve and **cleanse** the circulating blood. Its natural **phytochemicals**, including **flavonoids** and **anthaquinones**, are the active ingredients, and make it an important plant to grow in your garden. You don't often see it in the supermarket and it can be costly, but it will grow brilliantly in a decent-sized pot, and the more you cut it, the more it grows. As well as this tea, use it just like spinach in cooking and salads.

Ginger and Lemon Zizz

In terms of real physics, a cup of a hot drink when you're feeling freezing has about the same effect on your body temperature as adding a pint of boiling water to an ice-cold bath. But there's no doubting the psychological comfort of clutching a warm mug between your hands, sipping its contents, and inhaling the heady vapours. The difference here is that this drink really does "ginger you up" and gets those blood corpuscles fairly whizzing round your veins and arteries.

Serves 1

2.5cm or 1 inch root ginger
half a lemon

1 Peel and grate the ginger.
2 Put into an infuser or mug.
3 Add 200ml or 7 fl oz of boiling water.
4 Cover and leave for ten minutes.
5 Juice the lemon, reserving two slices.
6 Strain the ginger tea into a mug and add the lemon juice.
7 Serve with the lemon slices on top.

vital statistics

While we in the West consider ginger to be a warming, tangy spice that adds its wonderful flavour to both sweet and savoury dishes, Chinese herbalists have very different ideas. For 7,000 years, they've used it as an important medicine as well as a flavouring. The pungent **shogaols** and the stimulating **gingerols** and **zingiberene** have a dramatic effect on blood circulation, making this root a great **remedy** for poor circulation, chilblains, and Raynaud's disease. The **bioflavonoids** in lemon help by **strengthening** the blood vessel walls.

Sick-

After major surgery when I was a child, I was sent to a wonderful convalescent home in Surrey before I was allowed home and back to school. How sad it is that this whole concept of convalescence has vanished from modern health care! In the same way, few people who get sick seem to be looked after at home any more; they either struggle on or end up in hospital. It was always traditional to have a chapter on sick-room remedies in cookery books, but this practice has also vanished. Here, you'll find some of my favourite sick-room remedies that I've

room

Drinks

recommended to patients, friends, and family for the past
forty years. They'll help body and soul, revive the feeble, cheer
up the depressed, boost flagging energy, and strengthen the
body's natural defences. These simple recipes will help to
speed the recovery from minor ailments, reduce the
discomfort of unpleasant symptoms, and, thanks to the
mixture of fruits, vegetables, herbs, and spices, they'll soon
return you to your normal activities.

Liquorice and Cinnamon Booster

This wonderful healing drink combines some of the most ancient remedies known to man: soothing honey, the virtues of which were extolled in the Old Testament; lemons, a traditional cure for scurvy; cinnamon, a stimulant used in Indian Ayurvedic medicine; and the amazing properties of liquorice. For fatigue, coughs, colds, flu, sore throats, and even acid indigestion and heartburn, this is the first choice in the sick room.

Serves 1

1 piece of liquorice about
   1cm or ½ inch long
half a lemon
1 piece of cinnamon about
   1cm or ½ inch long
1 heaped tsp honey

1 Put the liquorice in a large mug.
2 Cover with boiling water and leave until dissolved.
3 Juice the lemon.
4 Add the cinnamon and lemon juice to the mug.
5 Stir in the honey.
6 Drink while still warm.

vital statistics

It's the juice extracted from the liquorice root that's commonly used in medicines and confectionery. Its medicinal value was recognized in 1,000BC, and its Latin name holds the key to its **benefits**. *Glycyrrhiza* is a combination of the Latin *glykas*, meaning "sweet", and *rhyza*, which translates into "root". The **essential chemicals** in the root are **antibacterial**, expectorant, and **healing** to the mucus membranes of the mouth and **throat**. In the stomach it creates a **protective** gel which prevents acid damage and relaxes the **digestive muscles**.

The Luck of the Irish

Carageen, the wonderful Irish moss, has an ancient history of both culinary and medicinal use. It is excellent as a vegetarian substitute for gelatine, and helps to set junkets, jellies, and blancmange. This surprisingly pleasant and satisfying drink is ideal for all stomach and bowel problems, and is an excellent remedy for heartburn and acid indigestion.

Serves 2

**2 heaped tbsp Carrageen moss
    (available from most health stores)**
2 tbsp runny honey
half an unwaxed lemon

1 Rinse the moss well and put it in a heatproof bowl.
2 Cover with cold water and leave for ten minutes.
3 Pour over 500ml or 18 fl oz boiling water.
4 Put into an oven on its lowest setting (110°C/225°F/ gas mark ¼) for about two hours, topping up with boiling water if necessary.
5 Strain and stir in the honey.
6 Juice the lemon, cut the rind into thin strips and stir the juice and rind into the moss mixture.
7 Serve in mugs or heatproof glasses.

vital statistics

The **vitamin C** and **antiseptic** properties of lemon and the soothing, **healing** value of honey are well known. More surprising, perhaps, are the medicinal **benefits** of this Irish moss. Rich in healing **chlorophyll**, **betacarotene**, and an abundance of **trace minerals** from the fertile Irish soil, it's a wonderful restorative during or after any illness.

Winter Berry Punch

Fruit is one of the healthiest and most life-supporting of all food groups, but berries come top of the class in the health-promotion tables. They're the richest sources of the protective antioxidants which guard every cell in the body, warding off damage and disease, especially cancer. Adding ginger and cinnamon gives a boost to the circulation as well as a lift to the spirits.

Serves 4
350g or 12 oz frozen or washed
  fresh mixed berries
2.5cm or 1 inch fresh root ginger
4 cinnamon sticks

1 Put the berries in a saucepan.
2 Add about 600ml or 20 fl oz of water.
3 Peel and bruise the ginger, but leave it in one piece, and add to the pan.
4 Bring slowly to a simmer and continue simmering for ten minutes.
5 Remove the ginger and strain the liquid through a sieve, pressing the fruit to extract all the juices.
6 Warm through if necessary.
7 Serve with cinnamon sticks as stirrers.

vital statistics

This punch overflows with **vitamin C**, **carotenoids**, and an abundance of cancer-fighting **phytochemicals**. The natural pigments that give the berries their deep-red, -blue, and -purple skins are some of the most **powerful** of all **cancer-protective** substances, which is why blueberries, blackberries, strawberries, raspberries, and blackcurrants feature so widely in all healthy cookery.

Peas, Please

This is a sort of instant pea soup – and just what's needed for anyone feeling a bit under the weather, miserable, depressed, anxious or suffering from seasonal affective disorder (SAD). Frozen peas are ideal for this delicious tonic, as they're quick and easy to prepare and lose very little of their nutritional value. Canned peas, on the other hand, lose much more vitamin C and are also generally high in salt. The spring onions and the mint add extra essential oils to boost resistance and energy levels.

Serves 4–6

2 large spring onions
350g or 12 oz frozen peas
1 large sprig of mint
**850ml or 30 fl oz stock made with
    low-salt commercial cubes or, far better,
    use the recipe for Veggie Mug on
    page 18**

1 Wash and trim the onions.
2 Mix with the other ingredients and warm gently in a saucepan until the peas are tender.
3 Reserving two tablespoons of peas, liquidize the stock mixture, adding boiling water if necessary.
4 Serve with the reserved peas floating on top.

vital statistics

Any form of extended stress, anxiety or depression drains the body's vitamin B stores, and fresh or frozen peas are an excellent source of **vitamin B$_1$** and **folic acid**. They also provide useful quantities of **vitamins A and C**, and fatigue-fighting minerals **zinc** and **iron**. **Antibacterial** and **antiviral** compounds in the onions help fight infection, making this an extra-valuable remedy for depressing infections like flu.

Dandelion Coffee

If we don't dig them up, mow them down or poison them, we let our domestic pets loose all over them. What a tragic fate for the fabulous dandelion, one of the most valuable of all garden herbs and the easiest to grow! In France, you can buy the leaves by the kilo in any vegetable market; it's no accident that they call it *pis-en-lit salade* or that its country name in the north of England is a direct translation: "wet the bed".

Serves 2

dandelion coffee (available at good health-food shops)
milk or cream to taste

1 Following the packet instructions, add the appropriate amount of coffee and boiling water to a cafetière.
2 Leave to stand for at least ten minutes; dandelion coffee takes longer to brew than regular coffee.
3 Pour into mugs and add milk or cream to taste.

vital statistics

The dandelion root is an even stronger **diuretic** than the leaves, although the leaves are a very rich source of **vitamins A, B, and C**, as well as **potassium**. Dandelion coffee is traditionally made by grinding the dried roots, and it is probably the most acceptable of all the coffee substitutes. For swollen ankles and general **fluid retention**, this is one of the **safest** and **most effective** remedies.

Note: You can also add young, green dandelion leaves to salad as a spring blood **tonic** for the tired and **anaemic**. And the sticky, rubber-like substance in the stalks really helps if rubbed onto **verrucas**, **warts**, and **corns**.

Pain-so

The use of food as medicine is, I'm happy to say, increasingly widely accepted, even though it's 2,000 years since Hippocrates first said, "Let food be your medicine and medicine your food." Not surprisingly, the idea of food for pain relief isn't so widely accepted in this twenty-first-century world of ours, as we expect instant results, especially where pain is concerned. The downside of powerful analgesics is that they all, and without exception, have side effects. When you consider that, in the UK alone, 2,000 people die each year and 12,000 are admitted to hospital for emergency treatment as a direct result of taking one of the widely used non-steroidal anti-inflammatory drugs (NSAIDs), you might like to think again. Perhaps waiting an hour or so for your pain to diminish seems a much more attractive option.

othing

Drinks

Nature works slowly, and few of these drinks will be an instant success. But none of them will have even mild, let alone catastrophic, side-effects. Perhaps the time has come for us to reassess our priorities and stop being quite so wimpish about comparatively minor aches and pains. Thanks to modern science and technology, the skills of the medical pain expert are amazing, and the ability for doctors to control unimaginable degrees of pain – especially post-operatively and in terminal illness – are quite remarkable. No one in his or her right mind would want to turn the clock back to surgery without anaesthetics and all the other medical horrors. But before you take a powerful painkiller for cramp, toothache, a painful bruise or an uncomfortable sore throat, why not give one of these recipes a try? I know you'll be pleasantly surprised.

Parsley Tea

It must be an attitude unique to the British and Americans that consigns parsley to the undignified and certainly unjustified position of being little more than a decorative garnish. It's true that the European flat-leaf parsley may be slightly more chewable and palatable than the British curly variety, but both are delicious and deserve more than their usual ignominious end: the compost heap. If you're suffering the discomfort of fluid retention, this is definitely the herb for you.

Serves 1

2 heaped tsp fresh chopped parsley or 1 tsp dried parsley

1 heaped tsp runny honey (preferably organic)

1 Put into an infuser or large mug.
2 Leave for eight minutes before straining.
3 Add the honey and stir vigorously.
4 Serve immediately.

vital statistics

Apart from significant quantities of **vitamins A** and **C**, **iron**, **potassium**, and **calcium**, parsley has a specific medicinal property that was recognized by the ancient Greeks and Romans and used by their physicians. This herb is a **gentle** yet effective **diuretic** and a real boon to the many unfortunate women whose periods are preceded by days of painful **swollen** feet, **ankles**, fingers, **hands**, and **breasts**.

Marmalade and Ginger Tea

Ginger marmalade is a great British tradition, and a similar concept to a British teatime favourite, rhubarb and ginger jam. In both of these recipes the ginger is added for its piquant flavour. But using ginger in food dates back to the kitchen medicine of the early Christian monks, who knew the healing and pain-relieving properties of this wonderful spice.

Serves 1

1cm or ½ inch fresh root ginger (dried ginger doesn't work)

1 tbsp organic thin-cut orange marmalade

1 Peel and grate the ginger.
2 Put into a mug or infuser and fill with boiling water.
3 Leave for five minutes and strain.
4 Add the marmalade and stir until dissolved.

vital statistics

You may find it surprising that even after turning bitter oranges into marmalade, the peel retains some of the healing **bioflavonoids**. Adding ginger to this tea releases all the **essential oils** and other **phytochemicals** from the fresh root. These directly **stimulate** the circulation and at the same time have a **warming** effect on the whole body. Whether it's a **headache**, arthritis, **rheumatism**, bruising or sports **injuries**, this drink will soon have you feeling better.

Rum-Rum, Chilli-Chilli, Rum-Rum

I suppose you could say that a generous tot of white rum has some anaesthetic effect, but that's not what provides the real benefits in this delicious, tropical-tasting, hot drink. Surprisingly, the chilli is the key ingredient, even though it's the coconut that provides the smell of the Spice Islands.

Serves 2
1 small red chilli
300ml or 10 fl oz coconut milk
4 tbsp white rum

1 Bruise the chilli gently.
2 Put into a saucepan with the coconut milk.
3 Bring slowly to a boil.
4 Strain into two heatproof glasses to remove any chilli seeds, add the rum, and serve.

vital statistics

Chillies contain an extraordinary ingredient called **capsaicin**, which is a very powerful circulatory **stimulant** and an effective **analgesic**. It was much beloved of herbalists for centuries, but used now as a prescription medicine by doctors, it can bring great relief to **arthritic joints** and injured muscles. It's also one of the few treatments that help relieve the pain of **chilblains** and **Raynaud's syndrome**.

Starry, Starry Peach

Peach juice is extremely good to drink, but watch out for cartons or bottles labelled "peach nectar", as these will have large amounts of added sugar. Although peaches are an excellent source of health-giving carotenoids, they don't possess pain-relieving properties. In this recipe, it's the star anise that will help you overcome the discomfort of abdominal distension and flatulence.

Serves 2
4 star anise
500ml or 18 fl oz peach juice

1 Put the star anise into a small bowl, cover with boiling water, and leave for five minutes.
2 Gently heat the peach juice.
3 Add the star anise and its liquid and simmer gently for five more minutes.
4 Pour into two heatproof glasses, leaving the star anise on top as a decoration.

vital statistics

Nutritionally speaking, juicing your own peaches as you use them provides by far the best results. They're not hugely nutritious to start with, but the fresher the juice, the more **vitamin C** and **betacarotene** you'll get. The **essential oils** from the star anise help to disperse wind in the stomach and colon, and so reduce **distension** and **pain**. Star anise is also good for the **relief** of dry, painful **coughs** and bronchial **congestion**.

Austrian Chocolate

Even if it had no pain-relieving properties, this heavenly drink – a variation on the favourite hot chocolate of Viennese coffee shops – would distract you from your discomfort and imbue you with sensations of peace, calm, and happiness. What could be more self-indulgent than wonderful chocolate, whipped cream, and spices? All this, and it's a pain-reliever, too!

Serves 2

1 organic satsuma

85g or 3oz good organic milk chocolate, like Green & Black's

½ tsp ground cinnamon

425ml or 15 fl oz milk

125ml or 4 fl oz whipping cream

2 pinches freshly ground nutmeg

2 cinnamon sticks

1 Finely grate the zest off the satsuma (eat the flesh while you're making the drink)
2 Break the chocolate into small pieces.
3 Put both ingredients into a saucepan, along with the ground cinnamon and two tablespoons of milk, and heat very gently, stirring continuously, until the chocolate melts.
4 Add the rest of the milk, continue heating gently until just boiling, and pour into mugs.
5 Whip the cream until stiff and add a heaped tablespoon to each mug.
6 Serve immediately sprinkled with nutmeg and with the cinnamon sticks stuck into the cream.

vital statistics

This drink isn't an analgesic in the pharmaceutical sense, but it is a major bringer of the **feel-good factor**. It is this sensation, which overrides the pain impulse, that makes you feel **positive** and **relaxed**. The **theobromine** in the chocolate and the gently hallucinogenic properties of the **myristicin** in the nutmeg generate these feelings – but the rest is **pure enjoyment**.

Rela

In our twenty-first-century, twenty-four-seven world of extended
working hours, hustle, bustle, and rush, relaxing is something the
majority of people now find extremely hard to do. Apart from feeling
guilty about not filling every available minute with some form of
activity, we're constantly bombarded with endless stimuli in every
conceivable guise: inescapable background music; the stresses of
family life and bringing up children; TVs that are never turned off; the
blinking eye of the cursor on the computer screen; the never-ending
stream of phone calls, text messages, and e-mails. The fear of being
"out of touch" has made people so paranoid that many are never
separated from their mobile phones, which are never turned off. Is it
surprising, then, that the skill of relaxing is fast disappearing from
Western society? The eternal adrenaline rush keeps us physically and
mentally prepared to act at every instant. But the fright, flight, or

xing

Drinks

fight reflex is no longer a reaction to emergency; it's a constant state of hyper-arousal, with all the risks that entails. Increased heart rate, raised blood pressure, rapid and shallow breathing, and permanent muscle tension increasingly take their toll with strokes, heart disease, bad temper, and constant aches and pains. Relief is usually sought in the medicine bottle containing sedatives, tranquillizers or behaviour-modifying drugs – all of which, of course, have side-effects. Most of them are, at best, habituating and, at worse, addictive. But don't panic: there is an alternative. You'll find it in the amazing bounty of nature's food pharmacy: herbs, plants, and spices which, through their flavours, aromas, and natural chemical constituents, have the ability to counteract the remorseless grind of stress, tension, and anxiety. Relaxation is available here in the soothing and delicious hot drinks that make up this chapter.

Happy Christmas

Alcohol is often the first thing that comes to mind when it's time to have fun, enjoy a party, celebrate any special occasion or just put your feet up, unwind, and relax with friends. This drink gives you two bites of the alcohol cherry. Beware, though; although a drink or two may make you feel merry and joyful, chemically speaking, alcohol is a depressant. So take it easy and remember, you can have too much of a good thing.

Serves 18

1.7 litres or 3 pints Guinness (or other strong ale)

225g or 8 oz demerara sugar

6cm or 2½ inches cinnamon stick

1 unwaxed lemon

1 tsp freshly grated nutmeg

1 pinch ground ginger

425ml or 15 fl oz dry sherry

1 Put half the Guinness into a pan.
2 Add the sugar and cinnamon and heat gently until the sugar dissolves.
3 Slice the lemons thinly.
4 Add them to the pan with the spices, sherry, and the rest of the Guinness.
5 Heat gently and serve warm.

vital statistics

Apart from the obvious pleasures of alcohol, beer provides ample quantities of **B vitamins**, which are essential **nourishment** for the entire central nervous system and help prevent and even **relieve depression**. In addition, the stimulating **essential oils** in ginger, the mood-soothing effects of cinnamon, and the great feel-good factor from the **phytochemicals** in nutmeg make this the perfect **relaxing** drink.

Lavender Barley Water

Lavender is one of the all-time-great herbal relaxants. Although you may be more used to using it as an externally applied oil for aches and pains, as granny's remedy for headaches or a luxurious and relaxing additive to the bath, this herb is delicious in food and drink. Combined here with the wonderfully soothing properties of honey, and the relaxing effects of barley, this is the ultimate relaxing drink.

Serves 2
As the preparation time is so long, double or triple the quantities, keep in the refrigerator, and warm as required

20g or ¾ oz pot barley
2 heaped tbsp finely chopped lavender leaves
2 tbsp lavender honey

1 Put the barley and lavender into a saucepan.
2 Add 425ml or 15 fl oz freshly boiled water and simmer for ninety minutes.
3 Strain through muslin or a very fine sieve.
4 Reheat if necessary.
5 Stir in the honey before serving.

vital statistics

The natural **carbohydrates** in barley and sugars in honey combine to make this an effective **stimulant** which encourages the brain to release soothing **tryptophan**. There are more than forty naturally occurring phytochemicals in lavender, including large quantities of the **healing** and relaxing volatile **essential oils**. As well as a relaxing drink, this is also useful for toothache, headache, migraine, **indigestion**, and **insomnia**.

Orange and Camomile Cup

Throughout the Mediterranean, most mothers know how quickly camomile can calm the most irritable, agitated, and fractious child. But it works just as well for adults – especially when combined with the soothing benefits of honey and the calming fragrance of orange blossom.

Serves 1

1 tsp dried camomile or
   one camomile tea bag
1 small or 2 large oranges
1 tbsp orange blossom honey

1 Put the herb or tea bag into a saucepan.
2 Pour over 125ml or 4 fl oz boiling water, cover, and leave for five minutes.
3 Meanwhile, juice the orange(s).
4 Strain out the herb, reserving the liquid, or remove the tea bag.
5 Pour in the orange juice and warm through.
6 Pour into a mug or heatproof glass and stir in the honey to serve.

vital statistics

One of the most striking characteristics of camomile is its wonderful fragrance. Just inhaling the **essential oils** has a direct and **calming** effect on the **brain**. This explains the wide use of camomile lawns in Elizabethan times, as the long skirts brushed the flowers and released the **oils**. If you ever visit Kew Gardens on the outskirts of London (and you *must*), go to Queen Elizabeth I's herb garden, where you'll find a stone bench covered in camomile. Ten minutes in the sun sitting on this seat will be one of the most **relaxing** times you've ever spent.

Basil Tea

Think of basil and most people's minds immediately conjure up a picture, the smell, and the taste of a wonderful, ripe, Mediterranean tomato. The flavours go together like bread and jam, but few people would think of enjoying the taste of basil on its own. Believe me, it's a great oversight – as you'll find out when you try this tea.

Serves 1
fresh basil: 3 large stems,
plus 2 leaves for garnish

1 Put the basil stems into a saucepan or infuser.
2 Pour in about 250ml or 9 fl oz boiling water.
3 Cover and leave to stand for fifteen minutes.
4 Strain into a mug and serve decorated with the basil leaves.

vital statistics

Basil is one of the great ancient herbs, native to India and the Middle East and grown around the Mediterranean long before Christian times. It was used by classical Greeks and Romans in both food and medicine, and was even thought to be a **holy herb** in the Greek Orthodox tradition. Medieval herbalists used it to relieve **headaches** and **stimulate** the brain, and just smelling the aromatic oils stimulates mental awareness. The special oils **linalool** and **borneol** are **mood-enhancing**, calming, and **strongly relaxing**.

Lime-blossom Milk

For those who aren't overly keen on the flavour of soya milk, the lime flowers and cocoa powder in this drink add their own distinctive tastes, which few people find unpalatable. This is an excellent drink for women finding it difficult to relax in the days before and at the beginning of their periods. Its calming action is thanks to the different phytochemicals present in each of the ingredients.

Serves 1

125ml or 4 fl oz soya milk
1 lime blossom tea bag
½ tsp cocoa powder

1 Put the soya milk into a saucepan with the same amount of water and bring to a boil.
2 Put the tea bag into a mug and pour on the soya mixture. Leave to brew and then remove the tea bag.
3 Serve with the cocoa powder sprinkled on top.

vital statistics

The hormone-like natural substances in soya milk help even out the ups and downs of the **hormonal system**. This is true regardless of whether the disturbances are cause by the menstrual cycle, breast-feeding or the menopause. Lime blossom is one of the traditional European teas that help bring **peace** and **calm**, and the **theobromine** in the cocoa powder is one of nature's most powerful **mood-enhancers**, which helps overcome **stress** and anxiety.

Bay Watch

The ancient Greeks and Romans revered the bay tree, and this member of the laurel family gets its Latin name, *Laurus nobilis*, from the Latin words meaning "praise" and "famous". This is the reason why laurel leaves are such a symbol of success in sport and the arts – but woe betide you if you're tempted to rest on them.

Serves 1

125ml or 4 fl oz milk
115g or 4 oz fromage frais
3 bay leaves
3 pinches ground cinnamon

1 Put the milk and fromage frais into a saucepan and stir until completely combined.
2 Add the bay leaves, bring slowly to a boil, and simmer for five minutes.
3 Remove the bay leaves and serve with the cinnamon sprinkled on top.

vital statistics

The ancient Greeks knew well what a powerful effect bay could have on the human **mind**. Visitors who sought advice from the oracle at Delphi inhaled the smoke of burning bay leaves, while the priestesses who interpreted the prophesies of Apollo were given bay leaves to eat. The **soothing** powers of the bay are enhanced here by the **calming** effects of the milk and fromage frais, and the **aromatic benefits** of cinnamon.

Minted Yoghurt

I don't expect many of you would think of yoghurt as a relaxing drink; nor, for that matter, would you expect mint to have soothing properties. The most commonly used mint – peppermint – has a sharp, astringent, and stimulating aroma. But warm these two together and you'll find a delicious, nutritious, and gently relaxing mixture.

Serves 1

150ml or 5 fl oz live runny yoghurt
100ml or 3½ fl oz semi-skimmed milk
3 sprigs of fresh mint, preferably
 peppermint, plus 2 leaves for garnish

1 Put the yoghurt, milk, and mint sprigs into a saucepan.
2 Heat very gently for ten minutes.
3 Scoop out the mint.
4 Pour into a mug and serve with the mint leaves on top.

vital statistics

The milk and yoghurt provide **calcium**, which is naturally **relaxing** and also **stimulates** the brain's release of **mood-enhancing** tryptophan. The main ingredients of mint are **menthol** and **menthone**, and as well as being one of the best remedies for **digestive** problems, these natural plant chemicals are mood-enhancing and relaxing.

Se

In truth, there are no real aphrodisiacs or sexual stimulants other than the highly dangerous or illegal (or both). But in these pages, you'll find a fascinating combination of traditional and new ideas that will certainly help to set the scene. Of course, I take it for granted that you will exercise a modicum of common sense. It stands to reason that no man will be up to much after a plateful of pasta, a giant T-bone steak with all the trimmings, and a large wedge of apple pie and cream. Even less so if he has washed it down with a couple of bottles of red wine and four fingers of brandy. Women tend to be more sensible with regard to food, but indigestion, wind, and an uncomfortable distended stomach don't make the best of bedfellows. When choosing food before your night of passion, try some of the traditional aphrodisiacs, such as asparagus, oysters, mussels, clams, and other shellfish. Fruits like

xy
Drinks

pomegranates, passion-fruit, figs, peaches, cherries, and strawberries should also be on the list. When it comes to main courses, go for fish of any sort (but especially fresh or smoked salmon), and light meats such as poussin, pigeon or quail. Or try the most obvious of all fertility symbols – eggs – made into the lightest omelette with *fines herbes*, fluffy scrambled eggs with a hint of truffle, a dish of hard-boiled quail eggs with celery salt, or (if you're lucky enough to find them) the sensuous, creamy texture of gull or plover eggs. These are the ideal foods to combine with the sexy drinks in this chapter. Here you'll find aromatic herbs and spices, whose volatile oils soothe the anxious heart; fruits and vegetables, whose history sustains their benefits in matters of love; and cordials, conserves, and honeys which add to the sexual *frisson*. These are all you need to help you find your path into the promised land of love.

Sweet as Roses

Pink is the colour of romance – and romance, after all, is the most powerful of all aphrodisiacs. Throughout the Middle East, as well as in the England of sixteenth-century herbalist Nicholas Culpepper, the aroma, taste, and texture of roses have been used to heighten feelings of love and romance.

Serves 2

2 pink grapefruit
75ml or 3 fl oz rose water
rose petals for garnish

1 Juice the grapefruit.
2 Heat the juice gently in a saucepan.
3 Pour into two cups or heatproof glasses.
4 Divide the rose water between the glasses and stir briefly.
5 Scatter the rose petals on top to serve.

vital statistics

Using pink grapefruit for this drink matters; they're not only **sweeter** than the paler varieties, but also enhance the deepness of the colour. At the same time, their **vitamin C** content is very important to the **health** and activity of sperm. It's not just rose petals that play their part; rose-hips, too, contain the same **mood-enhancing** and aphrodisiac **essential oils**. Diluted rosehip syrup is a suitable substitute if you can't find rose water.

Elderflower and Lavender Kiss

Elder trees were known and used by the ancient Greeks and the Anglo-Saxons, and they are still popular today. In ancient times, growing elder outside your house was supposed to keep the witches away, but in this drink, it will certainly help attract the romantic intentions of the person you're sharing it with – witch or not.

Serves 2

300ml or 10 fl oz elderflower cordial, diluted according to the bottle's instructions

2 long stalks of lavender, preferably with young flowers

1 Pour the diluted cordial into a saucepan.
2 Cut the flowers from the lavender and reserve.
3 Add the lavender stalks and leaves to the cordial.
4 Bring slowly to a boil.
5 Strain out the lavender.
6 Serve in heatproof glasses with the flowers floating on top.

vital statistics

A very simple but delicious and effective drink with which to ply your partner. People seldom think of lavender as a culinary herb, as the traditional way of using this plant is as an aromatic oil, bath additive or room fragrance. As well as its renowned properties for the **relief** of **headaches**, it's a very mood-enhancing and **calming** plant, too. The elderflowers contain **rutin**, which helps **protect** and **strengthen** the tiniest **capillary blood vessels** which play such a vital role in the art of love.

Amaretto Cup

Almonds are an ancient and traditional aphrodisiac. Wherever they grow naturally, they're associated with sex, love, and romance. In ancient cultures they were treasured by chieftains, medicine men, and religious leaders. As Christianity spread through the Middle and Near East and southern Europe, so these wonderful nuts became linked with wedding ceremonies. To this day, almonds are part of the traditional food given to the guests at wedding feasts in many cultures.

Serves 2

300ml or 10 fl oz green tea made to the packet's instructions from leaf tea or tea bags

2 tbsp Amaretto

15g or ½ oz crushed almonds

100ml or 3½ fl oz double cream

1 Make the tea and either strain or remove the tea bags.
2 Pour into two heatproof glasses.
3 Add the Amaretto, but don't stir.
4 Add the crushed almonds to the cream and whip until it forms peaks.
5 Serve with the whipped almond cream on top.

vital statistics

Almonds are an extremely **rich** source of **protein**, **minerals**, and **vitamins**, but they also contain the heart- and circulatory-protective mono-unsaturated **fatty acids**. These help ensure **efficient circulation** and are aided and abetted by substantial amounts of **vitamin E**. The added bonus of protective **antioxidants** in the green tea makes this a wonderfully sexy drink.

Celery Special

From a strictly nutritional standpoint, celery is a pretty poor source of vitamins and minerals, although it does contain some folic acid and potassium. If you have the unblanched, green celery and you also eat the leaves, you'll get a modest amount of betacarotene, too. And yes, it's probably true that you use more calories chewing it than you consume by eating it – that's why it's every slimmer's friend. It's the other substances in both the seeds and the rest of the plant that give it the reputation of being a gentle aphrodisiac.

Serves 2

2 large heads of celery, with the leafy tops
1 tsp crushed celery seeds

1 Cut off the celery tops, reserving two sprigs, and the outer stalks. (Keep the hearts to use in salads or as a braised vegetable.)
2 Slice the tops and outer stalks, and put them with the seeds into a medium saucepan.
3 Cover with 600ml (20 fl oz) of water.
4 Bring to the boil and simmer for one hour.
5 Strain into heatproof glasses and serve with the reserved sprigs floating on top.

vital statistics

Much prized by the Roman physicians and equally popular with eighteenth-century European herbalists, celery is a **gentle** but effective **diuretic** and a treatment for kidney and urinary infections. The essential oils have a strong **calming effect** and help overcome **nervousness** and **anxiety** – just what you need in **intimate situations**.

Soya Milk with Saffron

Throughout the Mediterranean, saffron is regarded as an almost mystical herb. It has always been expensive and used very sparingly for its vibrant colour and unique flavour. A traditional ingredient of Spanish paella, its aphrodisiac properties are as sensual as the shellfish – which is why saffron is the most important component of this wonderful drink.

Serves 2

1 large strand saffron
500ml or 18 fl oz soya milk
1 tbsp runny honey

1 Add the saffron to a little of the cold milk and stir until almost dissolved.
2 Bring the rest of the milk to a boil, then turn down to a simmer.
3 Add the honey and stir until dissolved.
4 Mix in the saffron milk and simmer for one minute, pour into heatproof glasses, and serve.

vital statistics

The **saffronal** and **crocins** in saffron are what kick-start the **aphrodisiac** properties of this very different drink. When combined with the **phytoestrogens** in soya milk, the overall effect on the **hormonal** system makes this drink an extremely useful aid to a normal, healthy **sex life** – and it works as well for men as for women.

Nobody understood the importance of sleep better than Shakespeare. His plays are liberally sprinkled with references to sleep and dreams. I've always thought the most telling of them comes from *Macbeth*:

> *Sleep that knits up the ravelled sleave of care,*
> *The death of each day's life, sore labour's bath,*
> *Balm of hurt minds, great nature's second course,*
> *Chief nourisher in life's feast.*

And what life is it when, night after night, you toss and turn, sleep fitfully with troubled dreams, and force yourself out of bed to face the next day's labours? Limping through life on a crutch of sleeping pills isn't the answer, because their long-term use creates dependence, or even addiction, to some of the stronger medications. The quality of sleep these pills produce is poor, because you lose the normal cyclical rhythms of your sleep patterns, miss out on the rapid eye movement

epy
Drinks

(REM) phase, and probably don't dream anyway. Does this matter? Yes, it does, because dreaming is the body's way of sorting and downloading the massive amount of data that your brain has received during the day. It's a bit like good housekeeping with your computer, when you delete all the unwanted junk from its memory. Everyone experiences occasional bouts of insomnia, whether they're caused by pain, stomach-ache, a cold, flu, or getting over some physical or emotional trauma. Certainly there are times when powerful sleeping pills may be justifiable. But what most of us need is a helping hand to relax, de-stress, unwind, and overcome anxiety. These recipes are gentle but surprisingly effective, and, even if you're a chronic insomniac, why keep taking the pills if they obviously don't work? Just the fact that you're taking control of your problem and making up a drink that's going to help will give you a more positive outlook on your sleeping difficulties. Most importantly, don't be obsessed by the eight-hours myth. You only need as much sleep as *you* need – and these drinks will show you how to get it.

Vanilla Soother

It's no accident that milk-based bedtime drinks are popular throughout the world. Milk is one of the classic bringers of Morpheus, the Greek god of sleep. The unique flavours of vanilla and allspice come largely from their volatile essential oils, and their fragrance alone is both soothing and soporific.

Serves 1
150ml or 5 fl oz milk
140g or 5 oz fromage frais
5cm or 2-inch length of vanilla pod
1 pinch allspice

1 Stir the milk and fromage frais together until they are well blended.
2 Pour into a saucepan, along with the vanilla pod.
3 Simmer for ten minutes.
4 Remove the vanilla pod.
5 Serve with the allspice scattered on top.

vital statistics

Calcium is one of the most effective **nutrients** for overcoming sleep problems, and thanks to the milk and fromage frais, it's present in abundance in this nightcap. In addition, milk is another food that triggers the release of sleep-inducing **tryptophan** in the **brain**. The whole process begins when you inhale the **volatile oils** and their delicious **aromas** released by heating the vanilla and allspice.

Lavender Blue

In a fascinating experiment some years ago, patients in an old people's hospital were taken off their sleeping pills and their ward permeated each night with the smell of lavender oil from a fragrancer. Within a few days, all the patients were sleeping just as well and waking the next morning far brighter, more active, and without the "hangover" feeling that sleeping pills cause. Mixed here with orange blossom honey and orange flower water, lavender makes the most delicately flavoured, lightly perfumed, and delicious bedtime drink.

Serves 2

5 tbsp fresh lavender leaves
2 tbsp orange blossom honey
100ml or 3½ fl oz orange flower water

1 Put the lavender leaves into a saucepan.
2 Add 200ml or 7 fl oz water and the honey.
3 Heat gently, stirring continuously, until the honey is completed dissolved.
4 Simmer for one minute.
5 Strain into cups or heatproof glasses.
6 Stir in the orange flower water to serve.

vital statistics

Lavender has one of the longest histories of a herb with medicinal values. It gets its name from the Latin word *lavare*, meaning to wash. It was the Romans who used it to **perfume** their bath water and introduced it to the British Isles. The **volatile oils** in lavender have been known for centuries as a **gentle**, soothing **sedative** and the **soporific** effects of this drink are enhanced by the **essential oils** of orange and the **sleep-promoting** action of the honey.

Good Night, Sleep Tight

Valerian was much revered by the ancient Romans for its powerful medicinal properties, and it has been used by herbalists since the earliest days of medicine as a calming herb. Adding maple syrup imparts an interesting flavour, and also supplies brain-soothing carbohydrates from the natural sugars.

Serves 1

1 tsp dried valerian herb
1 tsp maple syrup
1 dash peppermint essence

1. Put the valerian into a mug or infuser.
2. Pour over about 250ml or 9 fl oz boiling water, cover, and leave for five minutes.
3. Strain the liquid into a clean mug.
4. Stir in the maple syrup and peppermint essence to serve.

vital statistics

Although this recipe uses the dried herb, the most potent extracts are made by herbalists from the large, radish-like root of this remarkable plant. The **phytochemicals** in valerian are antispasmodic, **calmative**, and **sedative**, making this tea an excellent sleeping draught and **remedy** for stress, anxiety, and **insomnia**. Peppermint is a bonus, as it's also **antispasmodic** and calming, in addition to its main medicinal use, which is for the **relief** of sleep-disturbing **indigestion** and heartburn.

Sultana Tea

The high content of fibre in bran helps prevent constipation and speed up the passage of food through the intestinal tract. This also helps to avoid indigestion, wind, and uncomfortable spasms of the bowel muscle – all of which are common reasons for disturbed sleep. The natural sugars, iron, and potassium in the sultanas help relieve stress and anxiety.

Serves 2
115g or 4oz sultanas
40g or 1½ oz bran

1 Chop the sultanas.
2 Put them into a jug, along with the bran.
3 Pour over 600ml or 20 fl oz boiling water.
4 Cover and leave to stand for about eight hours.
5 Strain, reheat, and serve.

vital statistics

Soaking the sultanas in hot water helps to extract the **sugars** and other nutrients which make this such a **sleep-friendly** drink. Additional **B vitamins** and **fibre** from the bran increase the calming effect and the brain's production of feel-good **tryptophan**.

Hops with Honey

You're probably already aware of how beer can be used to ward off the evils of insomnia, but in this recipe, we're really back to basics as this drink is made with hops. To extract enough of the soporific natural chemicals from the dried flowers, it is important that you leave them to infuse for at least ten minutes. Also, make sure you follow the instructions and keep the drink covered.

Serves 1

1 tsp dried hops

1 tsp heather honey

1 Put the hops into a mug or infuser.
2 Pour over 250ml or 9 fl oz boiling water, cover, and leave for ten minutes.
3 Strain into a clean mug.
4 Sweeten with honey to serve.

vital statistics

Hops, which give beer its **sedative effects** as well as some **vitamin B$_6$**, have a long and honourable tradition as a **medicinal** plant and they were highly **valued** by our ancestors. That is why you'll find them engraved on antique decanters and glasses and as decorative carvings over doorways and mirrors – they played an important part in early religious festivals. The only problem is they don't taste that good, which is why we've added the honey.

Sweet Dreams

What could be sweeter than this heavenly mixture of flavours and aromas? You only have to smell it to know how soothing this drink is – and it only takes a sip or two to realize how effective it will be at helping even the most dedicated insomniac to have a decent night's sleep. You may have to hunt for good lavender honey, but some of the best is produced in Norfolk, England, and Provence, in the south of France.

Serves 1

250ml or 9 fl oz buttermilk
2 tbsp lavender honey
3 pinches freshly grated nutmeg

1 Heat the buttermilk until just warm.
2 Add the honey and continue heating, stirring continuously, until the honey is dissolved.
3 Froth the mixture using a whisk or cappuccino wand.
4 Sprinkle over the nutmeg to serve.

vital statistics

Buttermilk used to be the sour milk left after butter-making, but today it's nearly always pasteurized skimmed milk with added cultures to make it thicker. It has a slightly acidic, sour taste and is an excellent source of **calcium**, **beneficial bacteria**, and some **protein**. Like all milk products, it's a good **sleep-inducer**, and flavoured with soothing lavender honey and the extraordinary **feel-good**, mildly hallucinogenic effects of nutmeg, one mug of this drink will help you look forward to wonderful dreams.

Barley Broth

Nothing like the apology for barley water you can buy as a cordial, this is the real McCoy. A long time sick-room favourite for urinary infections such as cystitis, it's also a great aid to a good night's sleep – and doubly valuable because, as well as helping you gently into the land of nod, it prevents the frequent night-time trips to the bathroom if you have cystitis.

Serves 4
55g or 2 oz pot barley
1 large unwaxed lemon
1 large tbsp honey

1 Add 850ml or 30 fl oz of water to the barley and put both ingredients into a saucepan.
2 Cut the lemon into thin slices and add to the pot.
3 Simmer for ninety minutes.
4 Strain, stir in the honey, and pour into cups to serve.

vital statistics

Barley is a very neglected grain, but it's a good source of **calcium**, **potassium**, and **B vitamins**. This most ancient of all cultivated cereals also has valuable amounts of **fibre** and, like all starches, helps trigger the release of the natural sleep-inducing chemical **tryptophan** in the brain. Honey is widely used in folk medicine as a sleep promoter and combines perfectly with the other ingredients to make this a most **pleasant** drink.

24-Hour Detox Fast

Why detox? A short, sharp twenty-four-hour detox fast is a great shot in the arm for your metabolism as it provides a quick boost to your white cell count and, consequently, your natural resistance. Following this simple plan gives your liver and digestive system a day off, recharges your growth and repair mechanisms, and, in spite of the headache some people may develop by the evening as their blood-sugar levels drop, leaves you with an overall sense of well-being, renewed vigour, and a surge of extra energy.

Detoxing is not about losing weight, but it is concerned with mental, spiritual, and physical cleansing. Do not follow this programme if you are diabetic, on medication that needs to be taken with food (nonsteroidal anti-inflammatory drugs, for example), or if you have any serious underlying medical condition for which restricted food intake is inadvisable. If you're not sure, then speak to your own health-care professional first before trying it.

The day before you start this twenty-four hour programme, do not drink any alcohol, tea or coffee after lunchtime, and in the evening have a light but delicious meal, ideally of fish, vegetables, salads, fruits, eggs or pasta. It helps if you avoid red meat, large amounts of cheese, and the local take-away. During the afternoon and early evening, be sure to drink at least six large glasses of water.

On waking
A large glass of hot water with a thick slice of organic unwaxed lemon.

Breakfast
A large mug of Apple Tea (*see* page 10) and a glass of water.

Mid-morning
A large mug of Lemonbalmade (*see* page 36) and a handful of raisins.

Lunch
Hot Banana Smoothie (*see* page 63) and a large glass of hot water with a thick slice of organic unwaxed lemon.

Mid-afternoon
Hot Tommy (*see* page 34), six dried apricots, and a large glass of water.

Early Evening
Chicken Yum-yum (*see* page 54) and a glass of hot water with a large slice of organic unwaxed lemon.

Mid-Evening
A large mug of Sweet Dreams (*see* page 119) and a tablespoon each of pumpkin seeds and walnuts.

Bedtime
Camomile tea.

Any headache you may have developed will be gone by the morning and you will wake up feeling refreshed, revitalized, and raring to go. Ideally, start the next day with a bowl of fresh fruit, a carton of organic live yoghurt, a thick slice of coarse, wholemeal bread with a scraping of butter and honey and a cup of your favourite tea.

Nature's Medicine Cabinet

Condition	Healing foods	Effect
Acne	Apricots Apples Elderflowers	Are rich in betacarotene, which is essential for healthy skin. Provide antibacterial vitamin C. Boost immunity.
Anaemia	Beef tea Beetroot Eggs	Is a good source of iron. Promotes healthy blood. Provide iron and vitamin B_{12}.
Anxiety	Bananas Nutmeg Lemon balm Basil	Provide vitamin B_6. Is a source of mood-enhancing natural chemicals. Promotes relaxation. Functions as a mood-enhancer.
Arthritis	Ginger Green tea Parsley	Works as a natural anti-inflammatory. Contains protective antioxidants. Is a diuretic that helps eliminate uric acid.
Asthma	Mango Cloves, cinnamon, and allspice	Provides betacarotene for healthy lungs. All improve breathing.
Bronchitis	Citrus fruit Chillies Ginger	Provides antibacterial vitamin C. Work as an expectorant. Is a natural decongestant.
Bruising	Tropical fruits	Provide healing enzymes.
Chilblains	Ginger, cinnamon, and chillies Limes and lemons	All improve circulation. Contain bioflavonoids for healthy blood vessels.
Cholesterol	Apples and pears Peanuts, almonds, and oats	Provide fibre that helps remove cholesterol. All lower cholesterol.
Chronic fatigue	Bananas and apricots All nuts Beetroot	Provide instant energy, potassium, and vitamin B_6. Are good sources of slow-release energy. Helps improve oxygen levels in the blood.
Cystitis	Parsley Cranberries Kiwi fruit	Is a natural diuretic. Are antibacterial. Provides immune-boosting vitamin C.
Flatulence	Mint and ginger	Relieve discomfort.
Fluid retention	Parsley and celery	Are both effective diuretics.
Heartburn	Live yoghurt Mint Milk	Provides probiotic digestive bacteria. Aids digestion. Neutralizes acidity.

Condition	Healing Foods	Effect
Heart disease	Purple grapes, blueberries, green tea, beetroot, dates	All contain heart-protective antioxidants.
Hypertension	Garlic Parsley and celery All nuts and seeds	Helps lower blood pressure. Are gentle diuretics. Provide extra vitamin A.
Influenza	New Zealand manuka honey Citrus fruit Ginger	Is naturally antibacterial and soothing. Provides flu-fighting vitamin C. Speeds up the elimination of waste products.
Insomnia	Basil and lemon balm Milk and milk products	Contain soothing and sedative natural oils. Stimulate production of sleep-inducing hormones.
Laryngitis	Sage and rosemary Honey Citrus fruit	Contain soothing and antiseptic oils. Soothes inflamed membranes. Supplies resistance-boosting vitamin C.
Menstrual problems	Soya milk Cherries Bananas Parsley and celery	Provides hormone-like phytoestrogens. Are a good source of extra potassium. Contain vitamin B_6 and potassium. Are diuretics that relieve uncomfortable fluid retention.
Mouth ulcers	Yoghurt Lemon balm, basil, and elderflowers	Contains natural bacteria that help heal and prevent recurrence. Are relaxing and stress-busting; stress is the most common cause of ulcers.
Raynaud's syndrome	Basil, ginger, garlic, and chilli	All help stimulate circulation and may relieve the symptoms.
Restless legs	Beetroot Dates Mango and pawpaw Beef tea	Improves the oxygen-carrying capacity of blood. Contain iron; anaemia is a common cause of restless legs. Provide healing enzymes. Is a good source of vitamin B_{12}.
SAD	Basil, lemon balm, star anise, and cinnamon Nutmeg Bananas, milk, yoghurt	All are mood-enhancing. Contains the feel-good phytochemical myristicin. All increase levels of mood-boosting tryptophan.
Sinusitis	Onions, garlic, and thyme Ginger, cloves, and chilli	Are effective antibacterials. Have expectorant and decongestant properties.
Varicose veins	Cherries, blueberries, and citrus fruit Ginger and chillies All nuts and seeds	Contain vitamin C and bioflavonoids for healthy blood vessels. Stimulate circulation. Provide vitamin E for healthy blood vessels.

Index